Jozef Kozár

Make money online and be free

by

Jozef Kozár

ISBN: 978-1719272001
First Edition. 2018
Self-published.

https://www.jozefkozar.com

Copyright © 2018 Jozef Kozár, Ph.D.

All rights reserved. No part of this book may be reproduced or transmitted in any form or by any means, electronic or mechanical, including photocopying, recording or by any information or storage and retrieval system, without written permission from the author.

Disclaimer: This book is made to provide a good information about the possibilities to earn a legal money online and to provide a motivation for self-employment. The author is not engaged in any legal or professional advice. The author and publishers specifically disclaim any liability that is incurred from the use or the application of the contents of this book.

Cover photo source: Pexels.com under the Creative Commons Zero License (CC0).

Dedicated to Alena and Ringo

Contents

Contents vi

Foreword 9

Let's begin.. 10

Explore the possibilities 13

Do only what you like and do some magic 15

Third-party options that already offer you possibility to earn money 17

Combine the magic with some available online third-party options... 24

Website or how to be online...................................... 26

Your first website 37

Become visible 49

SEO, or how do people find you............................. 51

Marketing strategy 53

And what next? 60

Interaction 63

Never give up 68

References and used resources:...............................70

About the author..72

The best thing that you can have is the freedom.

Foreword

Hello. You have open this book probably because you were curious how to earn some money online or how to become successful on the web. Thank you for trusting me in this matter, so lets' dive deeper into this topic.

Let's begin

Maybe you have already asked yourself the question "what should I try to do online to become successful". This is very good question, but then you probably ended up very quickly with some answers like there is almost everything online and nothing else cannot be even invented. And this is wrong. Because even when there is everything out there, you still can do what you like and you can do it much better than anybody else does. And you know why? Continue reading and you will see.

The first and the most important thing is that you must want. It is common phrase that everything begins with just a dream. And that's right. We all are dreaming about something and we all are doing some job to earn money for our lives. But the question is if you are happy with your daily life. Take a look on some simple math:

1 piece of full time working person

Full time work = **40** hour per 1 week

1 year has **52** weeks

So every full time working person spends **2080**

hours at work every single year. Or better said, you spend one fourth of your life at work. When we will say it in math, it is 25% of your life time spent for somebody else, for some corporation. And there are not counted any overtimes and time spent by travelling to work and back home. The question here is, are you happy that you spend your life for working for some company, doing probably something that you do not like so much and you must ask for anything you want? Imagine that you want to have some vacation, can you simply go home or stay at home, because you just want that? No. There is still somebody who has the power and you must ask that person. OK, many people are happy with this, but what if you have some other dreams? What if you want to become independent, free and for example if you can imagine yourself working whenever you want, wherever you want and just how much you want?

"Never leave your job unless it is necessary."

Now you can see how much time you spend with working for somebody else. Yes, you always work for someone else, unless you are independent and free. Of course, it is not such easy just to leave the job and then just begin your own venture. No, never do it this way. Remember, you must eat and sleep every day and every night and for this purpose you still need some money. The ideal case is when you build your own independent online job alongside your main job. The online job can still grow and you are not in any risk in that time. We can see it in a diagram below:

1. Phase of thinking, but still working in main job.
2. Phase of making notes.
3. Phase of researching the ideas and making decision what you can do online.
4. Phase of building a website, but still working in main job.
5. Phase of optimization, marketing and growing online.
6. Earning online and still keeping the main job.
7. Becoming free and fully independent with the online job.

The steps in the diagram simply means that you can invest the most important thing that you have – your time – into something that you like and that can even earn you money. When you will reach some critical point where you will realize that you are happy that your hobby is earning you money, then you are there! You are ready to focus on things you ever wanted to and you can work even from the beach. Or of course, from the mountains, if you like.

Explore the possibilities

There are really many things that you can do online. Even when you have not started yet, you can divide your possible activities in three separate categories:

1. Something that you like and with what you can do some magic
2. Online third-party options that already offer you some direct possibility to earn money
3. Combine the magic with some available online third-party options

If you decide for any of the options above, always keep in mind, that the following conditions will earn you money online.

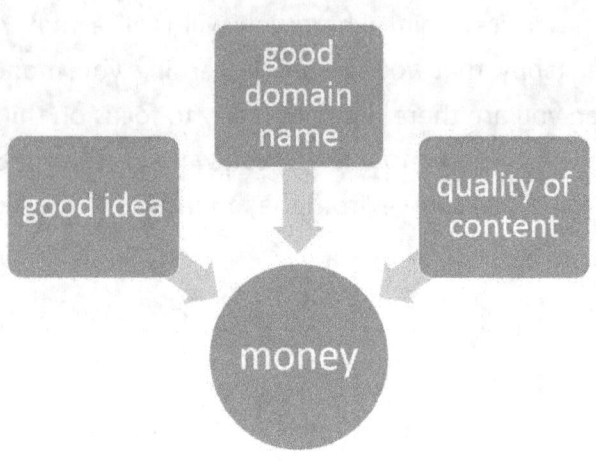

It means that the first must be an idea, which you probably know – it can be simply your hobby or the topic that you like most. About the good domain name we will talk later on next pages, but the very important is the content. Remember, even the bad looking websites can win the visitors and earn money when there is high quality content. The content means your text, photos, etc... But do not worry, you will be focused on your hobby and everybody is usually expert in her/his hobby, because when you spend time with something that you like, then I am sure that you know a lot about that topic. OK, let's take a look on the possibilities.

Do only what you like and do some magic

I can tell you that even I did some wrong decisions in my past years. I was one of those people who was focused on something that I did not like too much and I was always telling myself some excuses. Something like "do not be crazy, you cannot earn money with astronomy" or *"no way to earn money online with space technology and education"*. And the time was ticking. And still ticking. Until one day when I was taking a shower, I got an idea to try something different. I was in a part of my life when I was bored in my regular job, I have decided to finally find a job in the area of my hobby or better to say – in a totally different subject than my main job was at that time. So I started like other people, I just followed the well-known concept. Writing CV, sending the CVs to many HR agencies and trying to apply for my dream job directly in various companies. Although I had more than 10 years' experience for example in my previous job, I was not successful to get a job in the area what I liked. Nobody was interested in my courses or education or a lot of theoretical knowledge in my head. Probably because of lack of the practical experience in my dream subject of work, or probably because of something else. Who knows? And then it came. I put one to one in my head, I summarized myself that there must be some other way. There are many well-known people and they were once in the same situation like I was. And what they did? They never gave up! They just followed their dreams, not listening to others in the crowd saying that they are just dreamers. Yes. This is the way to become happy and successful. Do what you like, focus on your hobby and do it better than others do. In a single day you will change yourself from an amateur hobbyist to a respected professional.

And where is the magic hidden? The magic is called **quality**. Why quality? Yes, good question. The biggest possible quality can be achieved only by someone who loves the work she or he does. It simply means that when you will be doing something that you really like, you will never do it just because you must. You will do it because you like it and because it is your hobby. You will be then ever happier when you will see others happy from your product or service. And what can be a better advertisement than a happy customer?

Third-party options that already offer you possibility to earn money

Sometimes there are situations that you like – for example writing about travelling or just posting a photos on your blog. You may ask me here, how can I earn money with that? How can I turn a hobby like this into a money factory? The answer to this question is very easy. The answer is simpler than you ever expected. These days there are many big corporations out there on internet and they offer many services, products or anything else that earns money to them. So why not to join this ride and participate on their business? Ahaa! I can already hear your next question and you even did not say it! How can my small blog join a business of some corporation? Yes, you can. Because you are professional. Do you remember what we said before? You are somebody who is concentrating on quality of something that you really like. The answer for you is hidden under the name "**affiliate program**".

Affiliate programs are some kind of business models offered by big companies on the web. Imagine some big online store that is selling a books. Study their website and look for word "join our affiliate program" or something like "become an affiliate". Then follow up with registration, fill in your details (be serious here, I will explain later, why).

After registration you should be usually redirected to some kind of affiliate central (or dashboard), where you can manage your account, you can enter your bank account details, your tax details, contacts and select the products that you would like to sell. After selecting the products there should be usually generated a short code with easy steps how you can put it on to your website. When you will follow the simple steps and when the product is finally placed on your website or blog, then you just started your first online business. And this is not the end, this is just the very beginning.

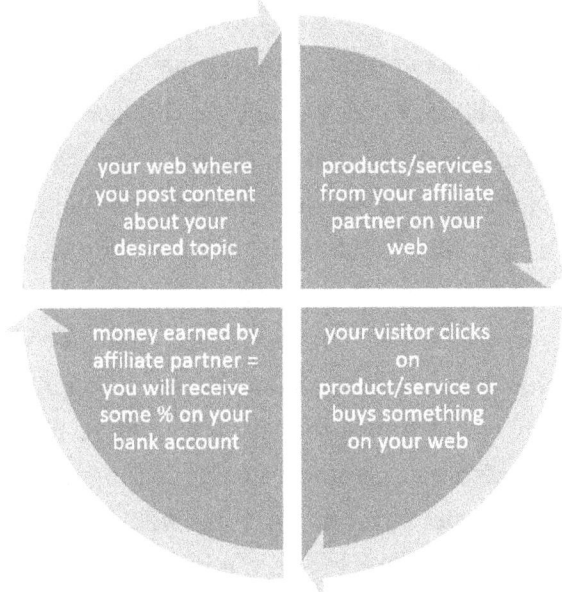

Every code of every product has its unique tracking ID. This tracking ID is usually a part of the code. You do not need to know the details, you just need to follow the instructions. Every affiliate program is almost the same, because it uses the same principles. It always wants to be as simple as possible. Because the providers of the affiliate programs know that when they want to sell as many products as possible, then they must allow also other sellers to offer these products. And how they can allow simple sellers to offer the products?

Answer is simple – to make it easy.

By selling of the products of some affiliate program will not make you any competitor to it. You are becoming their official partner and they are happy for that. They know very well that when you have a blog where you spend a lot of time focusing on quality of your posts, photos or all other content, then you will attract many visitors. And when you will offer their products, then there is rising a really big chance that their products are going to be sold. And when some customer – your visitor – will click on the product offered on your website or blog, she/he will be redirected to the original seller (your affiliate program provider). After successful purchase of the product, you will receive some amount of paid money directly on your bank account. Of course, the interest or the amount depends on the affiliate program. Some companies are offering quite nice amount, some of them no. It is always good idea to make some research first. I have searched for some interesting affiliate programs that you may like or with which you can maybe start.

For example, the best affiliate programs for the first months of 2018 are the following ones (according to independent research):

- TerraLeads:

  https://terraleads.com

- Clickbank:

  https://www.clickbank.com

- Rakuten:

  https://www.rakuten.com

- CJ Affiliate by Conversant:
  http://www.cj.com

- Amazon Associates:

  https://affiliate-program.amazon.com/gp/associates/join/landing/main.html

- ShareASale:

  http://www.shareasale.com

- eBay Partner Network:
  https://partnernetwork.ebay.com

- Affiliate Partners Ltd.:

  http://affiliate-partners.net

- CommissionFactory:

https://www.commissionfactory.com

- Avangate:

  http://www.avangate.com

- Flexoffers:

  http://www.flexoffers.com

- Avantlink:

  http://www.avantlink.com

- RevenueWire: https://www.revenuewire.com

- ReviMedia:

  http://www.revimedia.com

- AdCombo:

  https://adcombo.com

And what kind of products you can sell directly on your website or blog? The range of possibilities is really wide. At present you can sell books, products of daily use, airline tickets, hotel rooms, various services, advertisements (banners), almost anything. One special category may be some adult entertainment affiliate programs. But remember, be careful and be wise. Read every word mentioned in the conditions of the program you will choose and if you do not understand, then contact the respective support. If the affiliate program does not offer this option, then most probably they are not fair and you may not trust them. Avoid the problems, focus only on serious companies or programs. And always make everything in accordance to law. Every legal store or affiliate program will offer you an agreement that you must sign or just validate online.

And one very important note here. Do not forget, that when you are earning money, then most probably you need to pay some tax in your country. This may be different in any country and you probably know it how it works at your home. Usually the system is easy, the tax usually needs to be paid in the country of the person receiving the money or where you are an official resident.

Combine the magic with some available online third-party options

This is the third one from the list of the options. Imagine that you have a nice website, full of interesting content, many visitors and also that you are offering some direct services or your own product. Why not to enhance your services and products also with some products from some affiliate program? It can really happen that your customer cannot find exactly what she/he is looking for, among your own products or services. But this gap can be simply covered by some affiliate product. You will probably not earn from the sold item as much money as you would when you will be selling it directly, but you will still earn these three things:

1. You have a happy customer who will come back also in the future. Because your customer trust you and she/he knows that on your website or blog can be found many more products, that you are offering also your direct services and that you are offering also useful content with many advices, help, photos, reviews and many more.

2. Your website or blog is getting higher page rank in search engines, because you are directly connected to the large stores (your affiliate program) and they have most probably some kind of paid page rank (usually they spend a lot of money on marketing, advertisement, etc..)
3. You will earn a small amount of money from the sold product, because you did it for your affiliate program.

Ready to start? Do not hesitate, time is ticking and life does not wait. Your online money are just a click away from you.

One hint from my personal experience:

Before you will ever begin, take some notebook and write down the notes. Write down everything you are doing, because you never know. Some of your steps may not be something what you had expected before, but some of your decisions and ideas can make you a fortune. And there isn't anything worse than asking yourself "ah, what was the thing I did to make this happen?" or something like this "hmmm, what I wanted to do, what was that idea about?" – Personally me, I know that the best ideas come when you do not expect them. So write down everything. Do not forget your notebook and pencil anywhere you go. Take it with you.

Website or how to be online

Before we start with the following chapter, I will begin with some web design theory. I will explain you briefly what every magic word in web-world means.

Web presence or your domain name

The TLD (Top Level Domain) is much related to entire marketing and to everything else you will do in the future with your online business. The TLD is the name of the web address which your online web site or blog will use. For example the web address www.mybusiness.com is a name of the web address or your website or blog called "My Business". The words "top level" in the definition mean that the domain name is in the top of the hierarchy or in the structure of the web addresses in the Internet. The top level domains are the domains ending with .com, .net, .info, .org, .biz, and many others. Today there are many options which you can choose. The other type of the top level domain names (TLD) are the domain names of the specific country or region, for example: .co.uk. .us, .eu, .ca, .com.au, .cz, .fr, .asia and many others. Every internationally recognized country has its own top level domain. The international organization responsible for assigning the top level domains (TLD) is the organization ICANN.

What is not a top level domain? The domains like

www.mybusiness.freeblog.com

www.mybusiness.freewebprovider.com

www.freewebsites.com/mybusiness

Can you see the difference? These are called "second level domains". There are also ways to have a "third level domain" and these would look like

www.mybusiness.websites.freeprovider.com

or something similar. Can you see how your website would be "hidden" in the long address? So I recommend you – go for your own web address or better said, find your own top level domain. If you cannot find something you would like, the best practice is to use your own name and surname. You cannot damage anything with this choice and your online business will sound more serious – because you do not hide yourself, you offer everything directly under your own name.

Where to find a good domain name?

Personally me, I use the web services of *GoDaddy*, you can find them at www.godaddy.com. This service is one of the best out there on the web. After registration you are able to fully manage your domain name, you can transfer it to somebody else if you do not like it or you can do some other useful things with your own domain – for example forward it to other website. There are of course many other official registrars, where you can find your desired domain name. The full list of the official TLD (top level domain) registrars you can find directly on the official web site of ICANN:

https://www.icann.org/registrar-reports/accredited-list.html

Some hints from my personal experience:

When searching for a good domain name, think about the name of your business first. This name

should ideally match the domain name that you will use as your web address. Try to use something unique. If possible, it is very good idea to describe also your main services directly in you domain name. For example, if you want to offer some consultancy, then your domain name should look like www.idealconsultants.com or something with your last name www.lastnameconsultant.com.

Ask yourself directly "what domain name should I use?" Where you would like to focus your services – just locally or worldwide? If locally, then the best practice is to use the local domain name, like www.example.co.uk or www.example.de, www.example.fr, www.examle.us or anything else. There are many top level domains for specific countries or regions. But if you think that sometimes in the future you will expand with your online business, services, or just articles to the whole world, then definitely search for some universal top level domain name. I mean for .com, .net, .org, .info or for something similar. The reason is just practical. Your customers, or visitors of your website or blog will not be confused that the service or products are dedicated to some specific country.

Good and simple domain name makes your brand more trustworthy. So if you are unsure about some specific name, do not worry. Use a combination with your own First Name and/or Last Name. Remember, the best brands are always using the Last Name of their creators.

Internet

Internet is a digital world that is parallel to our own physical world. Do not laugh, that's true. There is no sci-fi anymore, no matrix, nothing special. Simply the digital reality. I will help myself with the citation from Wikipedia, to make it clear:

The Internet is a global system of interconnected computer networks that use the Internet protocol suite (TCP/IP) to link devices worldwide. It is a network of networks that consists of private, public, academic, business, and government networks of local to global scope, linked by a broad array of electronic, wireless, and optical networking technologies. The Internet carries a vast range of information resources and services, such as the inter-linked hypertext documents and applications of the World Wide Web (WWW), electronic mail, telephony, and file sharing. The origins of the Internet date back to research commissioned by the United States Federal

Government in the 1960s to build robust, fault-tolerant communication via computer networks. The linking of commercial networks and enterprises in the early 1990s marked the beginning of the transition to the modern Internet, and generated rapid growth as institutional, personal, and mobile computers were connected to the network. By the late 2000s, its services and technologies had been incorporated into virtually every aspect of everyday life. [1]

And here I think would be beneficial to mention some theory about the WWW, or to explain what exactly the World Wide Web is. The World Wide Web (abbreviated WWW or the Web) is an information space where documents and other web resources are identified by Uniform Resource Locators (URLs), interlinked by hypertext links, and accessible via the Internet.

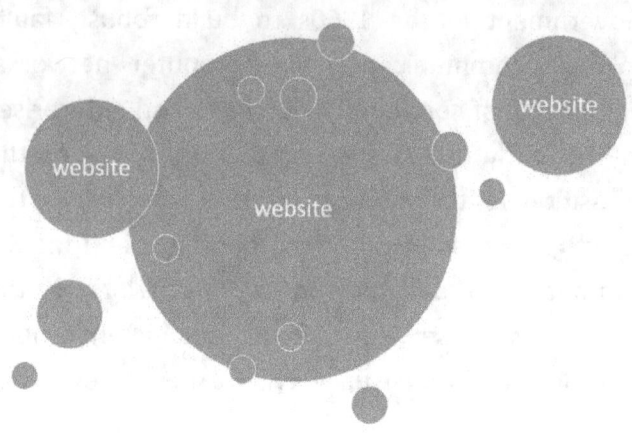

English scientist Tim Berners-Lee invented the World Wide Web in 1989. He wrote the first web browser in 1990 while employed at CERN in Switzerland. The browser was released outside CERN in 1991, first to other research institutions starting in January 1991 and to the general public on the Internet in August 1991. The World Wide Web has been central to the development of the Information Age and is the primary tool billions of people use to interact on the Internet. Web pages are primarily text documents formatted and annotated with Hypertext Markup Language (HTML). In addition to formatted text, they contain images, video, audio, and software components that are rendered in the user's web browser as coherent pages of multimedia content. [3]

URL

So now you know what the TLD, or top level domain means and also you know the brief history of the Internet and of the World Wide Web. Maybe you have already heard about something called "URL". This shortcut stands for "Uniform Resource Locator". Again some theory to make it clearer. Do not worry, it is nothing special. A Uniform Resource Locator (URL), colloquially termed a web address, is a reference to a web resource that specifies its location on a computer network and a mechanism for retrieving it. A URL is a specific type of Uniform Resource Identifier (URI). URLs occur most commonly to reference web pages (http), but are also used for file transfer (ftp), email (mailto), database access, and many other applications. For example most web browsers display the URL of a web page above the page in an address bar. A typical URL could have the form:

http://www.example.com/index.html

Which indicates a protocol (http), a hostname (www.example.com), and a file name (index.html). [2]

The example is shown in an image below:

So when somebody in the future will ask you *"could you please send me the URL of your website or blog?"* Then you just copy the whole "address" from the web browser and you will send it via email or chat.

Security of your website

This sounds a little bit scary, doesn't it? The online security is one of the most important aspects of these days. It is related to anything you are doing online – even when you are just sending an email to your friend or colleague, talking via some chat to somebody or when you are posting some articles, products or photos somewhere. There are some people who do not care about the security principles and they are putting their online existence – personal or business – into a big risk. Nobody wants to share the personal information or to lose anything business related. Can you imagine that some smart person will steal your money because this person will find some access details in your communication somewhere online? Yes, it can happen anytime. But do not give up, there is always an option to protect yourself and your online presence or business.

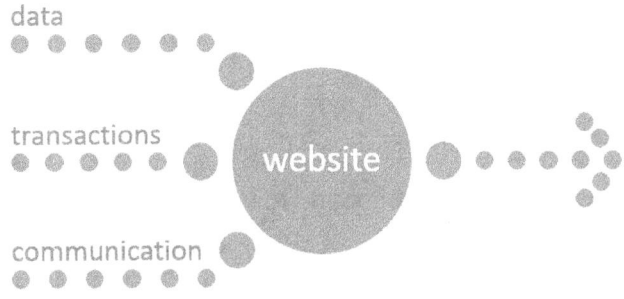

The most important one that will protect your website and all the online transactions that your visitors or customers will do on your web is to use the digitally signed security certificate. You do not need to sign anything personally, it is just the description of the service. This feature is becoming a standard in the online world among the serious websites that are protecting their activities. The security certificate means that your URL will look like something

https://www.mybusiness.com

instead of the unsecure version

<u>http://www.mybusiness.com</u>

Can you see the difference? The difference is the small "s" in the initial protocol description (http) at the beginning of the web address (URL).

When the website has the security certificate installed and enabled, then the URL will display this automatically. The security certificate can be obtained very easily directly by your web hosting provider. You just need to ask for this when ordering the web hosting. The most of the good providers already have this option implemented and you will be just notified after you will sign up in their system. Sometimes it can happen that this feature is not an automatic service and you just need to "tick" or confirm that you want it when you are ordering the web hosting. It may not be cheap, but there are also many free versions of the security certificates. So definitely go for this option and become safe online.

The security certificate means that every interaction between your website and the visitor is encrypted. The latest information from the major search engine providers say that the websites with security certificates (those with "https") are getting a better position ranking than those without the security certificates enabled. It means that the higher security can help you to jump in the search results to the higher places.

Your first website

Some of you probably understand the web design and all its dependencies and functionalities. Web design is a complex of activities, work, knowledge and theory necessary to successfully design, create and publish your website or blog online on the web. Here you have more options how to get to a website – you can design and create it yourself, you can ask some web designer or web design studio to do it for you, you can use some online – user friendly service to create your website and the last option is to use some ready blog platform to sign up for a blog.

Some of the above mentioned options have their limits and especially limited possibilities for doing business. Let's take a look on all of them.

Creating a website

Today the web design and the web technologies aren't such scary and complicated as they were a few years ago. After a short study of some online available materials, you should be ready to create your own website in a short time. For example, you can simply find some reliable web hosting provider that offers directly a possibility to install the content management system (CMS). After installation of the content management system you just need to log in with your own password and that's it. You are ready to fill in the website with your content (text, photos) and your website is immediately available online. I know, I have described this maybe very simply and you still do not understand what exactly I mean. So take a look on some details.

Static or dynamic websites using CMS

The technology of creating and operating of the websites may differ from one to another. In the past, most of the websites were static. What does it mean? Static website consists of the set of files, mostly HTML files, CSS, images and a few PHP scripts. The text content of the static website is written directly in the source code of the website. It means that every time when you want to update the text or some picture, you need to open the source code of the respective file of the website and then you need to edit it there. When you will save it locally, then you must upload the file to the web server and then the change appears immediately to the user. Of course, the user needs to refresh the website in the web browser – it will reload all the website's files from the web server.

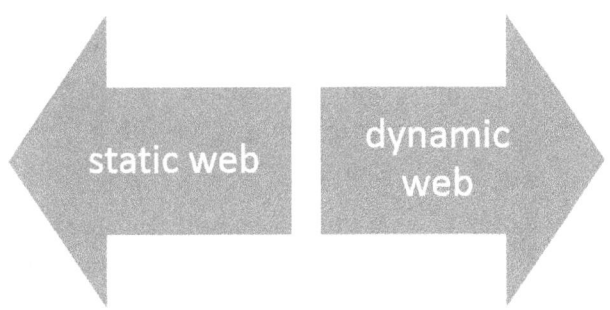

The dynamic websites are different. The content is separated in a specific files – these can be for example simple text files and images, or the content can be stored in the database (most common are MySQL, MS SQL, etc.). Dynamic website consists of the set of dynamic scripts – usually PHP files, ASP.NET, JavaScript files or some other types. I will not write all of them here, because the list would be pretty long. These are just the most common types. Of course, the dynamic websites have also some HTML files and CSS stylesheets. Creating a dynamic website from scratch is usually a little bit more complicated than creating a simple static website in HTML code.

And how do the dynamic websites work? Every time when user opens the website, the scripts that are the structure of the website, connect to the database set in the configuration of the website and then these scripts load the respective content – the text and images. Then the scripts "generate" the website and display it in the user's web browser. I know, maybe it is a little bit strange, why to make the websites this way. The reason is very simple. Imagine that you have a lot of text content, or many products that you would like to offer, This text content needs to be edited quite often – for example news, etc. Then you cannot have just a simple HTML static website. It is simply not manageable to perform changes very often. For these purposes are the dynamic websites. You just change the content in the background and it immediately appears in the foreground after user opens the website in the web browser. Do not worry, you do not need to know the programming techniques. We live in the 21st Century – everything is getting simpler every day. For the purposes of the dynamic websites there were invented the content management systems (CMS). The content management systems are the sets of files that make some kind of program package. When you would like to have a nice, flexible and dynamic website, you just need to do the few simple steps:

1. Obtain the web hosting and your domain name.
2. Upload the files of the content management system to your web hosting space (web server).
3. Open the web browser in your computer and just type there your domain name.
4. Your website will open – but not directly your website, but just the installation process of the content management system that you have chosen before.
5. Remember, from this point you need to read and just fill in the details. It is simple, but never skip anything without reading. To be honest, I did this few times and it happened

to me that I ended up in some kind of troubles. And I had to begin from scratch. But it was a couple of years ago. With modern content management systems like for example WordPress, you should not experience any problems.
6. During the installation procedure you will be asked to enter the details of your database – this you can find in the administrative dashboard of your web hosting provider. When you will log in there, you will have the option to create a database yourself, or probably your web hosting provider offers you directly some ready-to-go databases.
7. After successful installation you just need to refresh your website in the web browser and woohoo, here you are, your website is ready to use it.

I know, your website now does not look like you wanted to have it. We have just installed the content management system. The main feature of the content management system is, that it allows you to login to the background as an administrator, or web editor and from there you just need to type the text, insert pictures, and every other content you would like to publish on your website. You can later come back and change it anytime you like. Isn't it nice? This is the dynamic website and its main advantage.

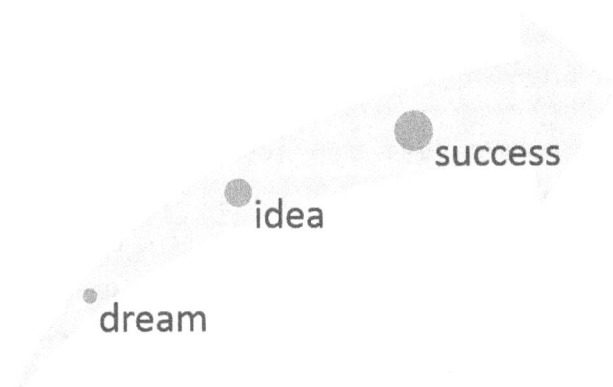

The look and feel of your website can be simply changed anytime you like. For every type of content management system that is currently offered by various communities or companies, you can find many ready to go designs. The modern content management systems allows you to search for any useful designs (often called "theme" or "template") directly in the administrative background. Just find the option in the menu called "look and feel", or "theme" or something similar. It depends on the content management system you have chosen.

As I have mentioned above, you can find many

useful and very stable content management systems. Personally me I prefer WordPress, which you can find at www.wordpress.org. This system has its own long history of development. It is very powerful, it contains many features and plugins and you can create excellent websites or blogs with it.

With WordPress can your website or blog become an e-shop, web portal, news portal, social web (imagine that you can have your own social network!) and anything else. And everything without the need of programming knowledge. This content management system you can install directly on your own web hosting under your own domain name or you can simply use the free available solution at www.wordpress.com.

After you will sign up for your own account there, you will get immediately your own website and your web address (URL) will look like www.mybusiness.wordpress.com. This is the second level domain name, but you can also use your own domain name here – there is a simple wizard that will help you step-by-step how to set it there. And you can directly use your website.

Other content management systems that I can recommend you are for example Joomla!

(www.joomla.org), Drupal (www.drupal.org) or if you need something simple, then for example the SilverStripe (www.silverstripe.org). There are also some other, but I do not have many experience with them. Although I used some of them, mostly I use WordPress for everything, even for a scientific websites that I need for my daily job (I am originally a researcher in space technology and planetary science).

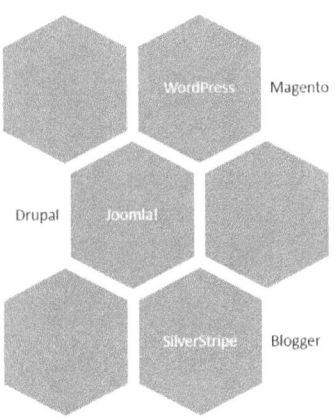

So you are maybe asking "what now?" or maybe you want to know the advantages of simple static websites and dynamic websites. At present the simple static websites are usually being used just for marketing purposes. For example if you have your main website for your business and you would like to make some single website dedicated just to one product or service and you do not want to mix it in the content of your main website. In this case you can choose the option to create the simple static website that will just promote the product or the service. Or there can be a situation that you are for example a taxi driver who does not need to have any special website, because you do not plan to make the changes of the content very often. In this case also, go for the simple HTML static website, put there everything you want and publish it on the web. In this case you do not need to waste your time by installing a robust content management system.

One hint from my personal experience:

If you want to have just a simple static HTML website that will be just promoting your services or something else, then you also do not need to know the programming techniques. You can simply download the ready designs, called templates. Just search the web for keywords "free web templates" or "free html templates" and you will find a lot of ready to go designs. Some of them are ready to use after a short registration on the respective server of their provider. You will just need to enter your details, the text, name of the website and your website is ready to publish once you save it!

What is a difference between the website and blog?

OK, this question may sounds to be a little bit tricky one! But in fact, there are some important differences between a website and blog. So, lets' take have a look on them.

The main features or functionalities that make the difference are the content and interactivity with visitors (your potential customers). A website is some static web consisting from other static pages offering some formal content – for example products or services. Blog is something different. It has interactive content that changes – there is at least one or two fresh new articles published every week. Blog offers a possibility to visitor to discuss about the content. It allows the visitor to add her/his comment usually under the each article. The articles are being published in time order – usually the newest are as first. There is a possibility for blog owner to add some products to the content of the blog, but blog itself is a platform focused more on fresh and quality content which people can read and where people can find the answers to their questions in form of useful information. On the other hand the website offers just the products, services and is focused more on promotion of the business, person, services or products.

So the border between these two is very thin. There is one very useful and effective solution to combine both advantages of website and blog. The best platform to make this is to use WordPress. This content management system allows you to build your online presence in one place. WordPress allows you to create your static content promoting your business or yourself with the pages functionality and with the blog section where you can publish frequent articles with the posts functionality. This way you can offer your visitors a fresh content in a form of fresh articles in your desired time-cycle, for example once per week. And on the same platform you can build the static pages describing your services or products. Or if you are building your own professional web presence, you can see the example on my personal website at www.jozefkozar.com – the "page" or the static content you can find in the top horizontal menu where I am describing my research and my work.

But the interactive content you can find on the bottom left side. There are some new posts published every few days. Hey, do not laugh, I know, sometimes I am busy so it is not a few days.

To make some conclusion, or my advice for you here, is to build your web presence using WordPress. It can bring you a homogenous and elegant look and feel just in one package. The optimization or later-content editing options are very easy and flexible. WordPress offers you really many available plugins that you can simply install to the content management system. And you do not need to know anything about programming. All you need to know is just to read and fill in the details.

Become visible

Very important thing is to be original and unique. What does this mean? Someone once said that there is almost everything on the web today. Yes, that can be true, but the question is how it is presented or how it is available to others. And of course, the quality of the content. Remember, when your website or blog offers only copied content from other webs, it means that your visitors will come, they will spend a short time on your pages or posts. And the visitor will probably never come back. Why? Because ask yourself. How will your visitor find you? Through the internet search engine. And do you know how the search engines work? I am sure that you know. When your visitor searches for something then she/he writes the phrase to the search field and the search engine offers the results. The list of web sites or blogs with the searched phrase. And can you imagine that one of them is yours and the offered bit of content is exactly same like on many others? Yes, on many others. The Internet is full of web sites that have just copied content from the others. So the best practice is to be original and unique. It does not matter that you write about the topic that was already mentioned somewhere. You must write it in your words. Make it original. Your visitors will want to know your opinion and they will definitely read it. And the most important thing is that they will come back. Back to your pages and posts in the future. And what is the best thing for any business? Happy and returning customer.

SEO, or how do people find you

In the previous chapter we have talked about how to become visible online among others. We have talked about the quality and originality of your content. This is much related to something called SEO, or Search Engine Optimization. SEO means the steps necessary to make with your website or blog to be optimized for search engines. This optimization means to make the content — text, images, and videos — that way, which the search services will be able to find, crawl it, index it and then offer it to the user among the found results. It is important to be indexed and not to be banned of course. So never put any illegal content on your website or blog. And also never copy any content from other websites or blogs. It is considered as plagiarism, so the search engines may mark your website or blog as banned or risky and will not include you among the results.

If you think that it is important to be among the first ten of the results that the search engine offers to user, then you may be thinking wrong way. Why? Because the strategy and the algorithm of each search engine is usually secret and changes quite often. And the first results may be just paid. The search engines are just service provided and owned by some company. And the company uses its resources as investment, they are looking for money. It is business for them. So the first tens of found results can be simply paying customers. And you can do any optimization of your website or blog, you cannot get among them without paying to search engine company. This is just my experience and knowledge. So focus on content, on its quality. Every user interested in the topic you are publishing about, will easily find you. Some useful hints for optimization of your website or blog:

- Link to other web sites. Talk to other bloggers or website owners and exchange the links with them. They will publish yours and you will publish a link to them. The best way is to make some section on your website or blog called for example "our partners".
- Register your free accounts with some interesting web portals offering similar services and describe yourself as detailed as possible and do not forget to put there your web address. Most of these web portals are very well indexed by search engines, so they

will find directly also your website. Use some keywords in the description and do not forget – the same keywords you should use also on your personal website.
- Write a description to each photo or picture published on your website.
- Never use too many keywords, even when it is possible. Remember, it is always better to use few, than too many.
- And again, be original. This is the most important.

Marketing strategy

Your website or blog is alive, anybody can find it now online and you are just waiting. Time is ticking and you see that nothing happens. You are just working on the content, writing texts, taking photographs and videos. And then you ask yourself, what is wrong. My answer to you is – nothing. The above mentioned is just not everything you must do. How will your potential visitors and customers know that you are the new on the market? You must let them know. Take a look at the diagram below.

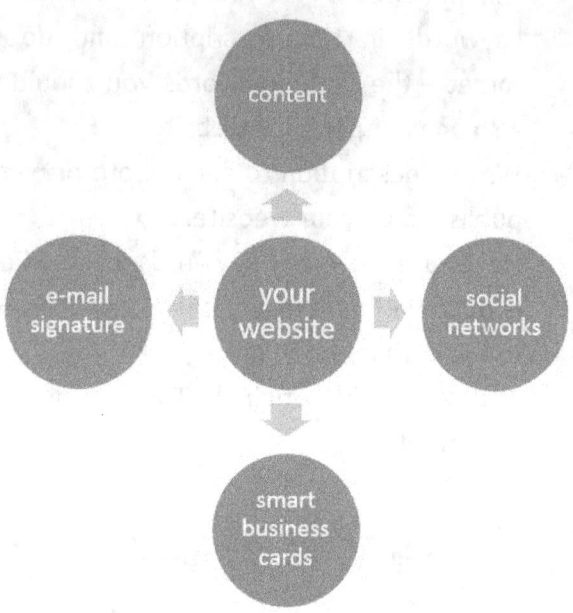

The diagram above simply describes what else you should do to let others know about you. As I have mentioned before, the most important is the content, its originality and quality.

Social Networks

The second important and very powerful marketing channel is to use the social networks to spread the words about your website. Always be professional and never forget that you are going to use the social network for your own project. You are not going to feed the social network with your content. All you should do is to be clear with what you share and not to share too much. Always share just a piece of your content with a strong focus on the link or address pointing to your own website or blog. People interested in your topic will definitely follow you and they will appear very shortly as your own visitor or potentially – customer. Remember that they must be happy with what they will find on your website or blog. Because they will share their thoughts and feelings to others on the social network where they initially found you. And this can even make an avalanche of new visitors for you or it can do something different when your content is bad or very poor on quality. But I am sure that you will do your best, because when you have come with the reading of this book to this page, then it means that you are enthusiastic and willing to work on your own project. So I am wishing you a good luck here, you are on the correct path!

Business cards

When you are at home, then you do not need

them. But the thing is, that you are a living person and you need to move. Especially when you want to have a successful website or blog. You must be hungry for new information and content. I am sure that you are planning to visit some exhibitions, markets, nature, museums, galleries, companies and that you are going to talk to other people. Many of the people you are going to meet in your near future are going to be professionals from your or other background. And what if they will ask for some contact or simply for some information about you and your website or blog? Here we go! You must offer them some information, because they are your potential visitors, customers, or they will spread the information about you to others. But how will they do that if they will forget maybe 50% of the information what you told them? Very easy answer – you will need some business cards. Do not worry, you do not need to put there your name, telephone or address. Use just simple calendar style business cards – these are small, on the rear side can be located small calendar and in the front can be very short description of your services with clearly visible web address. One hint regarding the very short description – never use anything strict, like you can see on other advertisements or business marketing materials. These are boring and people are ignoring them. Try to be creative here, use something more "chilly". You know, people are very curious, when you will write something that makes their curiosity even bigger, they will definitely try to find the answer directly on your web address mentioned there. And here we go – you have more visits that will generate you more money. Remember, visitors on your website are your customers. Now we have them inside the shop (your website is always your shop, even when you do not offer any products yet) – we now just need to make these customers curious enough to buy your service or to make them want your services. But before they will make you some money, they should enter your shop or even know about you. And can be there something worse than not having any contact information in hand when talking to somebody outside? Imagine that you are in some café, restaurant, or at some other event. You never know who you can meet and to who you would talk. And if this person asks for some contact or details? It is always worth to have some nice, interesting business cards. One interesting hint or piece of experience – what if somebody loses your business card somewhere? Bingo, you never know who will find it and who will read it. So do not worry. Just use the information on the business card that you think should be appropriate. Never use any exact personal details. Name, web address and some official contact (not personal) is more than enough. Never use postal address, you do not need that. Your business is online.

E-mail and Your Signature

Your website or blog is your own online business. If it is not focused on earning money yet, it does not matter. You never know when it becomes you own full time job. So my advice for you is to set up your own professional e-mail that you will be using for all communication to your visitors and later to your customers. You can even set up more e-mail addresses or accounts. It depends simply on you and on your own targets. And when you are sending any e-mail from your professional e-mail address, then always use some simple professional signature. I do not recommend you to use any graphics in your signature, because you never know how the e-mail will be open by the recipient or what kind of software will be used by the recipient. Each e-mail software uses different standards, so it may happen that your signature with your graphics will be just pasted as an attachment to your e-mail. And it can be considered by anti-virus programs like some spam or like some suspicious e-mail. So take a look below, this is maybe something that you should use:

YourName YourSurname

Your Website Name

www.websiteaddress.com

name.surname@websiteaddress.com

Remember that your e-mail signature is like the business card I have mentioned you in the chapter before. This is your digital identity card, your digital business card. You never know to whom it will be forwarded by your recipient. So be strict about your personal details here. But do not worry about sharing the useful information about your website or blog. But keep it always professional.

And what next?

Now we can say that you are ready. I am sure that now you are full of ideas. I hope that you have now a lot of energy to start. If you already started with your website or blog, than that's perfect. I am happy for that! But you are at the beginning. It does not matter if your website is for example 1 year old. Think always this way – "I am at the beginning". Do you know why? Because you never know what is waiting for you on your next day. You never know how your business will grow, what problems will come and how exceptionally you will solve them. Remember, there are solutions for everything you can imagine. Everything you need is to always keep the smile on your face and everything else will come. Because energy starts always with a good mood.

What I can recommend here is to set your daily work time, or some kind of pattern how and when you will work on a new content. We all are different, but we all should be professionals. If you will have some visitors, they will use to wait for the new content. They will have some expectations. And you did hard work to get the visitors, you must now do your best not to lose them.

Always think about the new ideas, new articles, new text content, photos or videos. Always take a piece of paper with you and make some notes when the idea will come. Do not worry, it does not look bad when you write your notes. It is very professional. And if you will write down your notes in some public place, then be sure that somebody will ask you what you are writing about. This is advertisement for you, give the person your business card. Remember, every activity that you do, can be simply your advertisement. You are communicating to public with everything you are doing. But just do it smart. Do what others are not doing (of course, only legal things!). For example the mentioned notes writing on public. Why not to have a note book with some colorful cover showing your website's name and web address? There are plenty of cheap online services where you can very easily design your marketing materials (pens, brochures, business cards, note books, caps, t-shirts, etc.), so try to use them. It is an investment for you that will come back to you as a reward very soon.

It is always very useful to write down the notes about your ideas. Because usually you will just keep writing and – here we go – you have another great article written and ready for use on your blog or website. Remember that writing the text on a paper has also some benefits for you. When you write the text on a daylight, you are definitely keeping your eyes healthy. It is still better to have everything ready on a paper and then just re-write it to the digital form on your computer. You can write your text on a paper also when you are sitting somewhere outside, in the park, restaurant, street and you will not attract anybody with your laptop. So you are even keeping you safe and also your equipment safe.

Many bloggers or website owners just give up their writing or taking care about their website very early. Because they are expecting that the website or blog will have a thousands of visits very quickly. But it takes time. Nothing is so quick. Especially the quality. It is a very good practice to make some work schedule and publishing schedule. For example mark in your calendar the time when you will be working on

1. writing the text and preparing other content (photographs, etc.) and

2. editing and publishing the content on the

blog or website.

Keep it periodic, do not give up. For example writing and publishing one great article every week is a very good example. Your visitors will know that every week there is a great content and they will definitely come back. And your visitors will be very soon your customers.

Interaction

Have you ever heard the word "interaction"? I am sure that yes, but lets' take a look how it can make a benefit for you. Imagine that you have published some very interesting content on your website or blog. Your visitors are reading the content, but they have some questions. Of course, they will find a contact section on your blog and they will contact you with the question. But what if there will be hundreds of the questions and you will not have enough time to answer all of them, or if there will be some question what you are not really sure about the correct answer? It is very simple. Interact with your visitors. Make some time for your visitors to answer those questions, but – do it online in front of the eyes of other readers. It is simple, just enable the discussion or comments below your content. Your visitors will use it for asking the questions and other participants (also your readers/visitors) will answer them. You can also answer to some of them, but you do not need to. A rich discussion can be sometimes more valuable than everything else. Because the visitors discussing under your text (or other content like photos, video, etc.) are simply contributing to the value of your online business. They will definitely come back in the future and the discussions will attract also other new visitors, because the web search engines will recommend it to them.

So the interaction we can simply describe with three words – work, fun, success. These three words are always connected, when your work is also your hobby. Your visitors and your customers will quickly recognize that you are doing your work with a passion and love. Because only true specialists and experts are doing the work this way.

Remember that your visitors are potentially your customers or they are the ones who spread a word about you – the best marketing or advertisement is the happy visitor/customer. So never be rude to any visitor that wrote any bad comment under your content. You do not need to reply to everything. Your visitors may not like everything that you have written and when you will show them the respect by not replying to them even when they have written something not very nice, they will come back in the future. And they will generate you the traffic (visits of your website or blog). So they will help you with their contribution to the discussion.

On the other side, try to read all the comments in the discussion under your content. Because some of the comments can be really helpful for you. Some visitors can share with you their ideas, advices or just some wishes what they would like to see on your website or blog. And this can help you to prepare the right content for them in the near future. They will be surprised and thankful. Even this will definitely help your online business to grow.

The information about what your visitors like most, is very important. Sometimes it can happen that people are lazy to leave a comment in the discussion under the content. But this does not mean that nobody had read it. Even in this case you can get the information what your visitors like most and what they are less interested. You can get this information by the simple analysis of the statistics of the website or blog visits. For this purpose you do not need to be a specialist for analysis, you just need to use some available tool for making a statistics of your web visitors. For this purpose I can recommend you the free and online available tools like Google Analytics or the project Piwik. You can use also the standard or default tool for visitors' statistics that offers you your website or blog hosting provider. This is a standard free service that is being offered by every hosting provider. These analyzing tools can offer you also the possibility to see the numbers of visits and will allow you to make some further, simple and anonymous analysis of users visiting your website – to know what they are looking for, what they read often, which section of your website or blog they visit frequently and what they are not interested in very much.

Never give up

OK, we have come to the end of this publication. But I am sure that you are just at the beginning of your new job. Of your own job where you will be free and independent. I do not promise you that you will get a lot of money (maybe you will!). But I promise you that you will spend more time with your family and that you will be more happy. Sometimes it can happen that you will be maybe tired or you will not have any ideas what to do. But remember, to be free you must always and everywhere "walk with your eyes wide open". The inspiration is everywhere. Only your strong will and endeavor can transform any inspiration to the success and money. And legally earned money will definitely make you more free than ever before. I wish you have a lot of ideas, will and a lot of success with your brand new independent job!

MAKE MONEY ONLINE AND BE FREE

References and used resources:

[1] En.wikipedia.org. (2017). Internet. [Online] Available at: https://en.wikipedia.org/wiki/Internet [Accessed 30 Oct. 2017].

[2] En.wikipedia.org. (2017). Internet. [Online] Available at: https://en.wikipedia.org/wiki/Internet [Accessed 30 Oct. 2017].

[3] En.wikipedia.org. (2018). World Wide Web. [Online] Available at: https://en.wikipedia.org/wiki/World_Wide_Web [Accessed 25 Apr. 2018].

MAKE MONEY ONLINE AND BE FREE

About the author

Jozef Kozár Ph.D., is a researcher in space exploration and planetary sciences. During his research and educational career he has designed many popular websites for students and general public. His personal attitude is to support the growth of the quality of the personal websites which are focused on education, science and business. Jozef Kozár believes in the freedom and positive thinking achieved by working in the dream job that each of us can once have. He believes that every enthusiastic person is a professional with a lot of useful knowledge that can earn money for her or his personal life. Especially in the new millennium when everything is online. This book contains Jozef's personal experience from promotion of websites and blogs with some useful ideas how to turn these experience and knowledge into the real and legal money.

Make Money Online and be Free

Jozef Kozár

First Edition.

All rights reserved.
This book, its text content, graphics and other content is an intellectual property of the author. No part of this book can be reproduced, re-published, copied, scanned or printed without a prior approval of the author.

ISBN-13: 978-1719272001
ISBN-10: 171927200X

www.jozefkozar.com

© Jozef Kozár, 2018

www.ingramcontent.com/pod-product-compliance
Lightning Source LLC
Chambersburg PA
CBHW052338220526
45472CB00001B/478